D1713090

THE PURPOSEFUL PURSUIT
OF PROFITS AND GROWTH IN BUSINESS

McKINSEY FOUNDATION LECTURE SERIES

Sponsored by the
Graduate School of Business, Columbia University

Blough—*Free Man and the Corporation*
Cordiner—*New Frontiers for Professional*
   Managers
Folsom—*Executive Decision Making*
Greenewalt—*The Uncommon Man*
Houser—*Big Business and Human Values*
Kappel—*Vitality in a Business Enterprise*
Mortimer—*The Purposeful Pursuit of Profits*
   and Growth in Business
Rockefeller—*Creative Management in Banking*
Watson—*A Business and Its Beliefs*

THE PURPOSEFUL PURSUIT
OF PROFITS AND GROWTH
IN BUSINESS

CHARLES G. MORTIMER

Chairman of the Executive Committee
General Foods Corporation

McGRAW-HILL BOOK COMPANY

New York   Toronto   San Francisco   London   Sydney

Textbooks on the art of management typically tell only part of the story of how to achieve success. The success of any business organization is perhaps as much a result of the characteristics of the chief executive as it is of organization structures, position in an industry, or of the other variables usually cited. The vitality, dynamism, and sense of values of the chief executive will, in due course, permeate the entire organization and give it direction.

Some of the characteristics and value judgments that Mr. Charles G. Mortimer has transplanted into the thought and practice of the General Foods Corporation during the past decade emerge vividly from this group of Columbia-McKinsey Lectures. His skepticism of the *status quo* and his spirit of "restless unsatisfaction" have made the seeking of a better way to do things a way of life in the company. Complacency and relaxed satisfaction seem to have had no place in his regime. It is this kind of spark and spirit that differentiates the successful from the pedestrian, the enterpriser responding to incentives and penalties from the bureaucrats operating in a network of rules and regulations.

While recognizing the essentiality of developing basic principles and policies to guide the company, he is also very much aware that they sometimes serve as screens behind which one avoids hard thinking and difficult decisions. These are the essential qualities for success in most organizations, whether they be business, governmental, or even educational. The scientists learned this lesson of critical questioning several centuries ago, but it has remained for leaders of business organizations, like Mr. Mortimer, to apply it on a broad scale as a daily experience in a large coordinated group effort.

It is one thing to set the course. It is another to make things happen. Since management in its bare essentials is getting things done through people, there must be a sense of involvement and commitment to the common purposes throughout the organization. Mr. Mortimer calls it "keeping the company in momentum" which he has sought to achieve by providing a system of challenge and reward, as well as commitment on the part of the company. ". . . The people who work for his company are investing their business lives as truly as stockholders are investing their money." He also acquired a nickname in the organization, "How-soon Charlie."

The ideas and the attitudes of the chief executive extend beyond the internal practices of a corporation to its relations to markets and to society at large. Business today is a stream of continuous activity, not a series of independent transactions on each of which an attempt is made to maximize profit. The concept of mutual benefit from transactions stands in sharp contrast to the formulation of the socialist's economics. "The quickest way for a company to help itself is to help its customers" and "the best way to make money is by helping someone else make money." A profitable volume is earned by first benefiting the consumer, and "this we do by reducing the price of our products whenever possible, and striving to improve . . . their satisfaction-in-use."

While much of what Mr. Mortimer has said so interestingly in these lectures is good solid sense that has been proven to be successful in the prosperity and growth of his as well as of other business organizations, strangely it seems to have limited acceptance by the business communities of some other parts of the world today, or even by segments of our own population. Some seem to make it an article of their faith to dissent. A careful reading of these lectures will disclose, however, why a growing and profitable business community is entirely compatible with, and beneficial to, the society at large that gives it sanction. What a valuable lesson these lectures could be for the lesser developed nations of the world!

There is still another thought that should be meaningful to those seeking the world's development. Mr. Mortimer is a marketer and hence most aware of the importance of marketing. Yet there is much validity to his admonition that the thinking and planning of manufacturers "must start at the consumption end of the stream of activity, rather than at the production end." On reflection, one realizes that most of the great business organizations of the world have developed by first developing markets, then providing supplies and manufacturing capacity to serve those markets.

The institutions and organizations of business are fully capable of enhancing the quality of modern life, both in terms of material abundance and cultural opportunities. Many of the guidelines to the achievement of these aspirations have been given to us by Mr. Mortimer in these lectures.

COURTNEY C. BROWN
Dean, Graduate School of Business
Columbia University

CONTENTS

CONTENTS

INTRODUCTION

It is not pointedly apropos, yet something John Quincy Adams once said somehow keeps coming to mind as this soon-to-retire corporate chairman undertakes an analysis of the consumer goods business he has headed and the role of the chief executive in its management and growth.

"A man's diary," the early-day President said, "is a record in youth of his sentiments, in middle age of his actions, in old age of his reflections."

I have never kept a diary, so this cannot be in any sense a "record." And I am confident that at least those who have reached or are nearing retirement under a mandatory-age policy will understand that I think of my views as being considerably fresher than "reflections"—rather as being recent, experience-founded convictions.

These convictions, based of course on far less awesome responsibilities than theirs, parallel what two Presidents of more recent vintage have articulated particularly well with respect to the responsibilities—and the lot—of any chief executive.

The late President Hoover said he had concluded that a few hair shirts were part of the mental wardrobe of every man. Then he observed, with what must have been conscious understatement, that "the President differs from other men only in that he has a more extensive wardrobe."

Anyone who visited President Truman in his White House office will remember that it was marked distinctively by a sign which read: "The Buck Stops Here."

Delicate Hoover subtlety or slangy Truman bluntness, the point comes through: that the ultimate responsibility for all major moves and decisions to insure satisfactory profits and to keep a business growing rests with its chief executive.

Always the pursuit of business profits and growth must be a *purposeful* undertaking. Attainment of this objective depends on how well the chief executive does his job of keeping his entire organization focused on his goal and moving purposefully toward it. And it should be underscored that the goal is two-pronged: today, profits; tomorrow a bigger, more prosperous business.

I propose to present this view of a business
4

through the eyes of a retiring chief executive who thus can set forth his philosophy and convictions almost without reservation. These will be the three parts of the presentation:

Part One will deal with the creation of a solid foundation for profits and growth. It will treat of the kind of company the chief executive envisions and go on to embrace the conceiving of its philosophy and policies.

Part Two will deal with motivating the organization and will treat the use of plans and techniques for doing an effective job.

Part Three will expound the bifocal approach to management. It will amplify one of the most valuable lessons this particular chief executive has learned during his many years of stewardship of one corporation.

The ideas which will be developed and the approach to be taken by the chief executive apply to all sizes of business. Even the smallest enterprise must have a chief executive, though he may not bear such an ambitious title, and any business will succeed better if it is operated with as definite a philosophy and as sound a group of principles and policies as though it were a billion-dollar corporation.

The fact that the chief executive of a small business lacks the organization and equipment of a large business may be one of his major advantages. Recently I came upon an intriguing statement in a book titled *The Sources of Invention*.[1] In a discussion of the fundamental discoveries which led to atomic energy, this point was made by one of the participating scientists: "We could not afford elaborate equipment, so we had to *think*."

Thinking is the basis of all business administration, and is not a matter of the size or sophistication of the enterprise. The purposeful pursuit of profits and growth must start—and end—with sound thinking.

CHARLES G. MORTIMER

[1] *The Sources of Invention* by John Jewkes, David Sawers, and Richard Stillerman, St Martin's Press, Inc., New York, 1958.

1

A SOLID FOUNDATION
FOR PROFITS AND GROWTH

*The kind of company the chief executive
envisions . . . Its philosophy and policies*

The first basic question confronting any new chief executive is: "What kind of company do I envision?"

He may not realize it at the time, but the day a man assumes the responsibility for the management of the company an important change takes place that involves *tense*. The subjunctive tense goes out the window of that new, plush corner office he has just moved into, and that little two-letter first word forever comes out of the *"If*-I-were-running-the company" phrase he had often used as he progressed up the corporate ladder.

For now he *is* running the company. And even as he enunciates the traditional open-door policy with respect to his ready availability, it isn't too early for him to close that door briefly—mentally, at least—and answer some self-imposed questions. Such as:

- Just what kind of company is this to be?
- What strengths inherited from predecessor administrations can we build on?

- What inherited weaknesses need special attention?
- What new philosophy, principles, or policies do we need to develop?
- How can company-wide enthusiasm be generated for the needed new concepts?
- How can we elicit maximum contributions from our directors—particularly the specialized knowledge and diversified experience of the outside board members?
- Is the top management group—and also the management further down the line—so deployed as to give the greatest impetus to the company's momentum?

In thinking through answers to these and many other purposeful questions, the new chief executive is subconsciously looking ahead in two ways. Humanly enough, he wants to make a real imprint on the company, so that when it comes time for him to retire, its good condition will reflect his contributions. Naturally—albeit not as a matter of early concern—this leads him to engage in a constant evaluation of his associates to decide, ultimately, which men might best be brought along as candidates to take over the top responsibilities when he leaves.

In the years it takes to evolve answers to these questions, the chief executive's leadership is effective in direct relation to the thinking he does and the pace he sets himself and his organization. And he must marshal and properly focus all possible imagination, resourcefulness, experience and ability throughout the company and so deploy it as to build the business soundly, solidly, speedily. He needs to realize early in the game that it is *his* responsibility not only to set the course but also to *make things happen.*

THE SPECIFICATION TECHNIQUE

The most effective way to set the course—and make things happen—is to specify, in some detail, the desired goals. These goals should be high, yet attainable. A vital first step is to apply a familiar technique to this never-easy task of reducing our ambitions to writing. The technique is one used extensively in the day-to-day carry-on of the business

—the *specification technique.* The very adoption of this technique conveys a sense of purposefulness to the organization.

In my company, after a good bit of time and the involvement of a great many of our best minds, we arrived at a basic specification for our business. It is a consumer goods business, with the many problems and potentials involved in dealing with the general public—and, specifically, with the distaff members of that public, God bless them!

Here are the seven articles of the General Foods basic specification:

1. A steadily growing company, with growth not based on size, volume, expansion or diversification, per se, but on consumer satisfaction created by the application of imagination, enterprise and skill to serving American homemakers with more and more products essential to their every-day needs, wants and convenience at prices that will provide reasonable and dependable profits on the funds, facilities, manpower and skills employed.
2. A company with farsighted plans for capitalizing on America's steadily rising standard of living, the expanding market for grocery products

at home, and the emerging opportunities in other markets of the world.

3. A dynamic company, outstanding in research in its industry, highly competent in production, aggressive and resourceful in marketing, efficient in distribution, economical in administration, and constantly reappraising its existing products, its share of market, its operating methods and procedures, its earnings and its progress.

4. A company offering challenging opportunities to men and women of character, skill and ability at every organization level, from routine jobs to high-level management positions; and providing immediate incentives and future potentials calculated to attract and hold people of outstanding capacity, ambition and drive.

5. A company cognizant of its role within its industry and as a part of the national economy; dedicated not only to "minding the store" well but also to advancing the interests of its industry and improving the national climate in which all business must operate.

6. A company which will earn profits at least as good as any company in the industry, thus permitting the steady payment of dividends, in good years and years not so good, in accordance with the dividend policy established by the Board of Directors.

7. A company occupying a leadership position in American industry and the world at large, widely and favorably known for the integrity of its products, the soundness of its policies, the fairness and friendliness of its human relations, and the capacity and vision of its management ... With high standards of responsibility toward its several publics: customers, suppliers, stockholders, employees, consumers, and the American people.

Such a basic specification must, of course, be revised from time to time as conditions require.

CHRONIC UNSATISFACTION

Emerging from the philosophy inherent in such a basic specification is a special attitude toward the profit-making function. This attitude—and it is of major importance—is what we have dubbed a spirit of restless *un*satisfaction.

Note that I do not say *dis*satisfaction. For *dis*satisfaction seems negative, and suggests disgruntledness; whereas *un*satisfaction is a reaching-up-and-out word—an expression of aspiration.

With an attitude of restless unsatisfaction, *status quo* becomes unacceptable in any area of the business. "Good enough" is never good enough. Thus, a wholesome measure of unsatisfaction becomes a valuable management tool.

It is unsatisfaction that leads to pioneering research, bold invention, resourcefulness, and the continuous improvement of products, production processes, and distribution methods which have characterized our country's incomparable progress. At whatever level of management, unsatisfaction can lead to finding better ways to make or sell a product; to greater awareness of what the consumer needs, wants or likes; to a private enterprise system unique in the whole world.

Restless unsatisfaction—with respect to practically everything—is a major article of successful management philosophy.

A story about a championship tennis match held some years ago in California epitomizes the importance of the spirit of unsatisfaction, and the way it can affect a company. As the story has it, the boy who won the title after a grueling match graciously accepted the congratulations of friends and spectators on his way to the clubhouse, and breathlessly arrived in the locker room eager to receive the one expression of approbation he valued most—the plaudits of his coach, the late, great tennis star, Bill Tilden.

But all he got was silence. "Aren't you going to congratulate me, Bill?" he asked.

"Congratulations," was all Tilden said, and rather grudgingly.

Perplexed, the boy asked: "What's the matter? I won the title, didn't I? I'm the new tennis champion."

"Yes," Tilden replied. "You won the title, all right. But today you played *not to lose*. To be a real champion, you have to play *to win*—always."

It is the always-play-to-win attitude which orients a company to peak profit performance. Profit orientaton means, particularly in a low-margin, high-volume business such as packaged groceries, keeping your eye on two balls simultaneously. Important as it is, increased volume is not enough; growth and overall company strength must be measured by *earnings* as well as *sales*.

In the quest for profit orientation in his organization, the chief executive will be well advised to remember, as he seeks profits today, that tomorrow is only a night's sleep away—if he can sleep!

A phrase used by the late Herbert Hoover highlights the very human side of administering a business. He referred to "the restless pillow of the manager." Nothing so aptly expresses his inescapable sense of responsibility to the people of his organization, the round-the-clock concern for them, which he carries on his mind and in his heart.

I include his heart advisedly. For while his mind is constantly grappling with the problem of earning profits for his stockholders, whose savings are invested in the business, his heart is charged with the welfare and job security of the company's employees. They are investing an important segment of their lives in the enterprise he heads.

He realizes that the great majority of these people have families to feed and educate, homes to maintain, insurance and mortgage payments to meet. And he knows the inseparable relationship between the level of his profits and the incomes of his employees, as well as the rights of his stockholders.

17

Another article, this, in the philosophy of a business in pursuit of growth as well as profits. For a business can grow only as its people grow and choose to invest themselves wholeheartedly in the enterprise which provides their livelihood.

The chief executive is responsible for creating an environment that makes his people *want* to grow, and helps them do it. In fulfilling this responsibility he will need to give his employees a thorough understanding of where the business is going. Especially he will be well advised to underscore characteristics that are unique to the business.

MARKETING—FROM PRODUCER TO CONSUMER

In a company which makes grocery products and markets them through to the consumer, for example, the chief executive needs to infuse the entire organization with understanding of the twin selling job that must be done. The grocery trade must be sold on carrying the company's products. Then, the homemakers of the nation must be sold on buying them. It is that kind of a business. With grocery shelf and freezer space growing scarcer every day as

18

new products vie for that space, it is just about as difficult to get products onto a shelf as it is to convince consumers to take them off, in preference to all the competing brands displayed side by side.

It was A. W. Erickson, founder of The Erickson Company, one of the predecessor agencies of McCann-Erickson, who crystallized this twin process succinctly when he stated: "It takes *selling* to start merchandise toward the consumer, and *advertising* to start the consumer toward the merchandise. The two forces meet in the retail store."

It is as simple as that, and as challenging, as was brought home to me early in my business career. It was back in 1924 when I was an eager-beaver assistant sales manager for the R. B. Davis Company, and part of my job was teaching young sales recruits how to sell baking powder. In those days, sales people did their own market research. Mine consisted of mentally measuring the width of the grocer's store door to ascertain how big a barrel of baking powder I should try to sell him.

I recall coming out of a little grocery store in a New Jersey town one day with an order for a relatively prodigious amount of baking powder, and with the compliments of an accompanying student salesman ringing in my ears. Suddenly, as I snapped my order book shut, it dawned on me that this grocer could not hope to move all the baking powder I had sold him in less than two years' time without promotion. In that instant, I recognized that I needed to know more about the all-important function of advertising to move goods promptly from grocers' shelves to their customers. It was this recognition of the concept of marketing as the process of moving goods from the producer all the way to the consumer that prompted me to leave the baking powder company and take a job for four years with a New York advertising agency to learn how advertising brings goods and consumers together. This experience, of course, stood me in good stead when I joined General Foods.

Today, the self-service retailer—and the grocery trade is almost entirely self-service—cannot afford to stock products that have not been pre-sold to Mrs. Consumer, usually by advertising over the air and in publications and other media. Such advertising involves the advertiser in pure feminine psychology, a realm that is both fascinating and baffling.

"WHY" AND "BECAUSE"

The difference between masculine psychology and feminine psychology is well illustrated by two of the simplest words in the English language— *Why* and *Because*. They might be characterized as sex words.

"Why" is definitely a man's word, sound, practical, probing, efficient. It suggests reason, logic, thoughtfulness, curiosity, exploration, elucidation.

"Because," on the other hand, is strictly a feminine word. It is the most ambiguous, beguiling, baffling, irresponsible, sweetly reasonable, completely unreasonable word in the entire lexicon of the fair sex.

Of the two words, "Why" is the older. It was first used by Alfred the Great, back in the year 888. It took 417 years—until 1305—for the ladies, bless their adorable femininity, to think up their diabolically sagacious and diplomatically evasive reply— "Because."

It took another 431 years for a man by the name of Nathan Bailey, who published a household dictionary in 1736, to make the perfectly obvious discovery that "because is a woman's reason."

21

Now if you think "because" is only a battle-of-the-sexes word, you were never more wrong. It is a tremendously important *business* word—in fact, a *dividend* word.

Every woman knows intuitively that there are three answers to a man's "Why?"

- The *rationalized reason*—which doesn't seem very important to her, but she can think up one if necessary;
- The *irrational reason*—which to her is perfectly valid and calls for no explanation or defense;
- The *real reason*—which involves tedious thinking and needless elucidation, so why bother?

It doesn't take long for a manufacturer of grocery products to discover that Mrs. Consumer's "because" leads her directly to the particular section of shelving in her supermarket where his product and his competitors' products are displayed side by side. Here her hand automatically reaches for his product —*or* a competitor's product. *Why? "Because."*

His business wins or loses a sale on her "because." His problem is to figure out *why*.

In the long run the annual earnings per share of a consumer goods business catering to the homemakers of America depend on discovering the *real reason* for Mrs. Consumer's "because," so the manufacturer can pound on it in his advertising—whether the real reason seems to him to be logical or illogical, rational or irrational. Actually, it will nearly always prove to be very sensible, once you get her slant on the product.

That is what makes it a *dividend* word. And that is why earning dividends year after year in a consumer products business is so challenging.

DOES ADVERTISING PAY?

The challenge to solve the riddle of "Why" and "Because" profitably is made all the tougher by the fact that conditions are far different than they were when Marshall Field was able to build a thriving business on the slogan, "Give the lady what she wants." Today, consumer expectations are so high and the pace at which new products are introduced is so fast that Mrs. Homemaker usually can't say what it is she really wants—until *after* some enterprising company creates it and she finds it in a retail store.

However revolutionary may be the new products which displace old, established products and usher in new habits of living and working, they often are neither immediate nor automatic in their impact. Even the best new inventions and the most obviously desirable new products have to be *sold*.

Persuasive advertising and aggressive promotion are the most economical tools for selling them. The faith business has in advertising—particularly those businesses where new products are all-important— is well illustrated by my own company's experience.

We spend millions annually in consumer advertising and promotion. I am sometimes asked whether this huge advertising expenditure pays. The answer is simple. It *has* to pay or we couldn't keep it up. Indeed, we have to get our advertising expenditure back with a profit within a reasonable period of time or we would go out of business.

Just *how* does our advertising expenditure pay? It pays by developing a large and dependable volume of sales.

But—and this is an extremely important point —we cannot earn for ourselves this profitable volume without first benefiting the consumer. This we do by constantly striving to improve our products' quality, convenience or utility—their satisfaction-

24

in-use—and whenever feasible, reduce their prices. And all this we must continually do if we are to make any progress in today's intensely competitive battle.

When we start to make up our marketing plans for the year, we do not say: "We will spend so-and-so-much for advertising." Rather, we ask ourselves, as the plan is made for the sales promotion of each individual product: "What will it take, in advertising and sales-stimulating inducements, first, to maintain the market position of this particular product (if it is already an established product) and, second (if we believe it to be possible), to increase the volume of its sales?"

If we are dealing with a relatively new product, we may ask ourselves: "How fast is it feasible to build volume for this new product, and what will such a rate of growth call for in advertising and other forms of sales stimulation?"

Usually, these calculations result in an advertising appropriation based on so many cents a case applied to the sales of the product, plus an experience-guided forecast of case sales we believe it will be possible to add by this promotion.

Thus the total figure for an upcoming year's advertising and promotion is not a figure pulled out of a hat, but a total appropriation arrived at by adding up the carefully-worked-out appropriations for each of our more than 30 brands and their even larger number of product varieties.

It is as simple as that—and as basic to profitable advertising.

HOW MUCH ADVERTISING IS ENOUGH?

I have been asked whether, after a product has been widely introduced through advertising, it is necessary to continue to spend so much for advertising, or whether, on the other hand, you can save on the cost of advertising by reducing the amount proportionately.

Obviously, the answer to such a general question will vary with the industry and the product being advertised. In the grocery business, however, the answer is a very emphatic "no" for three very good reasons. First of all, the job of acquainting the public with your new product is a never-ending one because of the changing and shifting market. For the past five years an average of 4,700 marriages have taken place in the United States every day. This means the beginning of approximately 196 new family units every hour around the clock. Fortunately, these new families are potential new customers for your product; but the bride is a brand-new shopper who has to be educated by persistent and persuasive advertising, for in effect, many times you are reaching her through your advertising for the first time that she has ever given a thought to buying such a product. Marriages and household formations are not the only changes in the market, but they represent a very important new opportunity to the marketer.

The second very important reason for continued advertising arises from the fact that you can frequently increase your volume of sales—in the case of consumer products, particularly—as readily by increasing the rate of use as you can by increasing the number of users. That is why in the case of a product like Jell-O, my company advertises persuasively—I hope—using pictures of mouth-watering desserts to coax Mrs. Consumer to serve the product more frequently. This job for advertising is a continual one, and it is a matter of arithmetic to justify the cost of the advertising by the volume resulting from the increase in number of users and increased frequency of use which you have been able to induce.

The third reason for continuing advertising may be the most compelling. Just as the consumer market is a constantly shifting one, so is the competition for the market. It is a constant struggle to cling to your precious position on the supermarket shelves. You remain there only so long as the turnover of your product justifies the choice position. Let up on your advertising, and some competitor will leap at the opportunity to capitalize on your weakness.

As a corollary of this last point, I would like to point out that a successful marketer is constantly reviewing his product to be sure that it produces the utmost in consumer satisfaction. He improves the flavor, or the texture or the directions for preparation, or he brings out an improved package with a fair degree of frequency. I cannot think of a single General Foods product which we were selling when I became chief executive eleven years ago which is still on the grocery shelves and has not been changed importantly and, of course, for the better.

There is no point to product improvements unless you bring them forcefully and persuasively to the consumer's attention through your advertising. You must try to persuade even those who may have used your product and not obtained sufficient satisfaction to repeat, that now it is well worth trying again.

The net of it is that to maintain and increase sales volume, a manufacturer must use advertising, first, to get the business started; and then—month in and month out, year in and year out—he must continue to use an amount sufficient to maintain and increase the purchases of the product.

One thing our long experience in advertising has taught us is that the surest way to *overspend* in advertising is not to spend enough to get the sought-for results. That would be like buying a ticket three-quarters of the way to Europe: you would have spent a lot of money, but you would not arrive at your destination on the Continent. This is just not good business sense.

SERVICE TO CONSUMERS—A BASIC CONCEPT

Thinking about the marketing of consumer products should not be focused too sharply on advertising and other forms of sales promotion. It is desirable that our perspective on marketing and distribution embrace the whole complex of operations and activities from the time a manufacturer assembles raw materials until they reach the ultimate consumer in the form of finished products. This includes production as well as marketing and distribution.

At first, "distribution" might seem to provide a sufficiently broad background for this complex, if defined as "the sum of all the arts which create a market for goods and services."

But this definition fails to suggest the revolutionary nature of the developments which underlie— and indeed precede—the "arts which create the market." And it omits entirely the important function of serving the public in the fashion to which it is rapidly becoming accustomed.

None of the numerous definitions of "marketing" and "distribution" I have read seemed to recognize what has happened in the past two decades to the business of serving Mr. & Mrs. Ultimate Consumer. They do not start far enough back in the involved procedures employed in the production of the revolutionary types of merchandise offered for sale today, and they do not recognize the extent to which heretofore undreamed of factors of convenience or utility are added during the processes involved in marketing and distribution today.

The lack of an adequate definition is probably one of the main causes of the wide criticism of "the high cost of distribution," and the frequently heard comment that industry has made great progress in cutting "production" costs but little in reducing "distribution" costs.

Old-time classical economists used to lump production, marketing, and distribution together as "production." But most of us of this generation are inclined to limit our conception of production to include only manufacturing processes and packaging. Customarily, we link advertising and selling under the term "marketing," and we think of the actual physical operation of delivery as "distribution."

Can we continue to do business with such a divided concept of industry's service to the public? I think not. Today it is almost impossible to say where *production* leaves off and *marketing* begins,

31

or where *marketing* leaves off and *distribution* begins. The three functions are so interwoven that they combine into one continuous flow of *service to the consumer*.

A few years back, the sales department of a company took the product from the production line and assumed responsibility for selling and delivering it. Today most products start, not merely with raw materials, but with a broad service-to-the-consumer concept, which is carried through a continuous stream of operations involving production, marketing, and distribution, with the product accumulating utility and value at various points along the way, until finally it reaches the ultimate consumer in its miracle form.

All told, in this stream of operations, each one necessarily adds its increment of cost as well as its increment of value. This needs to be stressed. This is the way raw materials are fashioned into some special form of usefulness or service to meet a consumer need or want.

Today's concept of production-marketing-distribution applies to *services* as well as to *products*. As services are accounting for a steadily increasing portion of the consumer's dollar, it is important that we recognize this fact.

ANTICIPATING WANTS AND NEEDS

Another way of expressing this concept of production-marketing-distribution is to say that in today's intensely competitive atmosphere, the manufacturer's thinking and planning must start at the *consumption* end of the stream of motions, rather than at the *production* end. Indeed, today's successful product or service is likely to start with a *consumer-use* specification rather than a *product* or *service* specification.

The old "mousetrap" theory, that if a man made a good product the world would beat a path to his door, has long since been abandoned as untrue. Marketing now *begins*, rather than ends, with a concern for what the consumer needs or wants. Today, the first step is to ascertain whether there are enough people who really want to trap mice to make the venture worthwhile.

The record is clear that the outstandingly successful companies are those which accurately and consistently *anticipate* Mr. & Mrs. Consumer's wants and needs and fulfill them as a logical next-step beyond existing living habits, desires, or expectations. No matter what type of product or service a business produces for sale, a new marketing factor must be reckoned with today.

To the old familiar terms, "consumer acceptance" and "consumer demand," a third must be added to the vocabulary of marketing—"consumer expectation."

Whether today's consumers passively *accept* new conveniences as characteristics of the goods and services they buy, or actively *demand* them, it is an inescapable fact that convenience in its many forms is coming to be *expected*—as a matter of course.

Assuming quality products and satisfactory service, the business which first provides the most convenience, in the most practical or acceptable form, at the best price, and promotes it most intelligently is pretty certain to get the lion's share of the market.

Creativeness and ingenuity are called for today as never before, not only in the design and production of goods and the development of services, but in their marketing and distribution. The manufacturer or producer, the merchant or purveyor of services, must meet the expectations of the consumer fully and promptly, or he will surely fall behind in the race.

HELPING YOUR COMPANY BY HELPING CUSTOMERS

In that race, where a packaged grocery product is concerned, there is, as I have stated earlier, a vital first lap—the contest with competitors to get your goods *onto* retail shelves. This you must do before consumers can even have an opportunity to take them *off* the shelves. So distribution is of the first order of importance in my company's concept of marketing, which we now see as everything which happens to the product between the factory door and the consumer's kitchen.

So we must continuously study our business from the distributors' point of view, making it our business to know *their* business and thus be better able to fulfill their needs—even anticipate them.

Indeed, one of the soundest lessons my years in business have taught me is that the quickest and surest way for a company to help itself is to help its customers—in very *practical* ways. The philosophy of helping the customer is obvious. It is the practicality that gives utility to the philosophy.

Let me cite three examples from my own experience by way of illustration:

Early in my tenure as chief executive, I headed a task force which took to the road for weeks on end and met with my opposite numbers and other high officers of most of our leading customer companies across the land. These meetings were no-holds-barred, and we urged our customers to tell us frankly about the shortcomings they were finding in our service to them.

Those meetings incubated a series of important actions which enabled us to get the jump on our competitors by providing improved delivery services to our distributors.

First, we conceived and instituted a market-centered sales and distribution system built on a nationwide network of combined district sales and distribution centers, with warehouses near our customers for prompt, efficient and economical customer service.

Next, time and labor savings were achieved—

both for us and our customers—by introducing a palletized shipping program which moves goods from our plants to our customers in unit loads, eliminating much manual handling. The pallets can be quickly and easily removed from freight cars or trucks, moved into the distributor's warehouse, and stacked. So far as I know, we pioneered in this method of shipping in the grocery industry.

The practicality of this approach is measurable. What we are doing is offering customers savings in *their* operating costs. A customer can save as much as $25 in handling costs in the unloading of a palletized rather than a deadpiled freight car. What does this mean to him? To earn an extra $25, a customer would have to increase his sales by more than $1,000. In the grocery business that means moving a great many more shoppers through his check-out counters.

The third step we took was to develop *individualized* sales and merchandising assistance, tailored to each particular customer's needs. Our sales staffs now provide customers with sharply-focused sales and marketing assistance and help our distributors move more of our products *out* of their stores more quickly to *their* customers, the ultimate consumers, so that their stocks turn faster. Again, very practical.

All three of these steps were taken, not out of altruism, but out of a sense of enlightened self-interest. For we know the growth of our business depends on having grocery distributors *want* to do more business with us, admittedly not from any special concern on their part for the success of our company, but because it is more profitable for them to distribute our particular brands.

William Feather, editor of the *Pickands Mather* magazine, boiled it down to a syrup when he wrote: "The best way to make money is by helping someone else to make money."

But no matter how practical or how profitable they may be, no business can coast on yesterday's projects or policies. Customer loyalty has to be *re-earned*, again and again, year after year. This means constant reviewing and revising of policies and procedures to keep them current with customer needs.

One of our more recent approaches to the well-being of our customers—and again, more than incidentally in our own self-interest—was the sponsor-

38

ing of an objective study, "The Economics of Food Distribution," made by McKinsey & Company at our expense, and presented to the grocery trade at a convention held in New York by the National Association of Food Chains.

This study was freely discussed at the convention by leaders of both the manufacturing and distributing segments of the grocery business. Subsequently, it was broadly distributed and discussed at many meetings of retail organizations.

This study-project illustrates one of the numerous ways in which a company can serve its customers for the very practical purpose of making it more profitable for both parties at interest to do more business together.

WHAT KEEPS EXECUTIVES AWAKE NIGHTS

Helping one's company by helping its customers is an important approach generated by the new type of competition today's corporate chief executive faces as he envisions the kind of a company he wants and proceeds to develop its philosophy and policies. Today's competition seriously undermines a chief executive's freedom of action, compared with the freedom enjoyed by the heads of yesterday's business enterprises. The profound change that has come about in the past decade or two in the area of business competition can be described in a sentence: *Competitors* have been superseded by *competitions.*

It used to be that the management of a business had only to worry about its *competitors*—the other companies in its industry. Today, in addition, it must worry about *three competitions:*

- The competition of other industries;
- The competition of scientific breakthroughs;
- The competition of swiftly and drastically changing public tastes, habits, and expectations.

Consideration of these three forms of modern-day competition emphasizes the point that our whole American economic climate would be vastly improved if critics who advocate limiting size in business on the ground that this will help competition could comprehend all the elements which truly make up competition—if they could see competition through the eyes of those who bear the responsibility for administering today's business enterprises.

What keeps chief executives awake nights just as often as keen price competition is the spectre of some competitor, big *or* little, coming out with a really significant improvement in his product or service—a superduper new model, a glamorous new style, a captivating package improvement, a patentable feature that provides a basic advantage, a new advertising or promotion appeal that really wows the consumers. And the bigger the business, the bigger the worry.

The first of the three current forms of competition, the competition of *other industries*, is a phenomenon that has grown up during the latter part of my own business career.

Once my own company needed to concern itself only with the competition of other food processors. Today, the drug industry has entered our field. Vitamins and such products as Metrecal are examples. The soap makers are barging into the food and beverage business on a major scale. The tobacco people are getting into the food act. And who can say what others will soon invade this area?

Steel companies, to take another example, used to compete only with other steel companies. Today, steel companies compete also with the aluminum industry and the even newer plastics industry—with the glass industry coming into the picture. And commercial banks, which once competed only with other banks, now face competition from outside— from insurance companies, savings and loan associations, finance companies and other firms. In short, practically every industry faces competition from industries that were heretofore no competitive threat whatsoever.

The second of the three competitions, *scientific breakthroughs*, is affecting a great many industries. This injects the competition of entirely new types of products which better serve old needs, and new processes which almost overnight displace old ones in which large sums of capital have been invested. One example will suffice. The new machines that make copies of all manner of business papers and documents in seconds have made a monumental dent in the use of carbon paper.

Finally, and perhaps the most baffling of all, is the competition of change in *public tastes, habits and expectations*. It took more than a generation for the public to lose its interest in horses and carriages in favor of the automobile. And it took another generation for commercial aviation to be widely accepted.

Today, the sophisticated traveler will capriciously switch his transcontinental flight from this airline to that one because on the latter's plane he can watch movies on a large overhead screen in the front of the cabin instead of on a smaller between-the-seats screen directly in front of him—or vice versa.

The consuming public is both independent and experimental. Old loyalties to products and services of all kinds are exceedingly hard to hold. Competition of a new scope, tempo, and intensity has developed which might be characterized as *triple-threat competition*.

This presents the chief executive of any business with tremendous problems—but also with tremendous opportunities. It all depends on how successful he is in guiding his business into the right competitive position—and so be *first to get to the top*.

But it also brings out the fact that he cannot manage his business in a vacuum. The conditions under which it must compete are so complex, and often change so swiftly, that he is no longer able to dictate—or even anticipate—just what kind of business he is going to be administering a few years hence.

He can, however—and he *must*—define what kind of company he wants to keep it insofar as its philosophy and principles are concerned. Its policies and methods are to a considerable extent affected by the new competitions. Nowadays, they must be more flexible than it ever seemed possible for the policies and methods of a company to be. In fact, it is imperative that the specification the chief executive writes for his organization's guidance be broad and flexible enough to encompass the three types of competition I have described.

For whatever satisfaction the chief executive can derive from the fact, he probably will find himself on both sides of tomorrow's competitions. He may be both the one being competed against and one of the new competitors barging in on other industries to try to win some of their business.

The chief executive who faces these new competitions may well take a leaf from General Grant's philosophy. When asked once whether he was never afraid as he led his army into action, Grant replied that he was nearly always afraid, but he counted on the opposing general being just a little bit more afraid than he was.

Finally, as he plans for the kind of company he wants his to be in the purposeful pursuit of profits and growth, a chief executive can be sure he will encounter moments when he will understand the feelings of the two cows that were grazing in a field alongside the highway when a huge aluminum tank truck rolled by. On its side was lettered: "Superior Milk. Pasturized. Homogenized. Irradiated. Vitamin-enriched."

One cow turned to the other and said, "Makes you feel kind of inadequate, doesn't it?"

2

MOTIVATING THE ORGANIZATION TOWARD PROFITS AND GROWTH

*Development and use of
appropriate management plans and techniques*

In fulfilling his responsibility—and a major one it is—to motivate his organization toward the pursuit of profits and growth, a chief executive can find a valuable assist in what Casey Stengel once said in that picturesque way he has of philosophizing ungrammatically but wisely. Asked by the press just before a World Series opening to comment on another pennant-winning season, the then-Yankee manager said: "I couldn't've done it without the players."

To get the most out of the players on *his* team, the chief executive needs, first of all, to comprehend that he is the chief custodian of the philosophy, principles, and policies of his company. Then he must shoulder the responsibility for the development and effective promulgation of appropriate plans and techniques that his management people will accept and can utilize profitably.

Many years ago A. W. Shaw, publisher of the *Magazine of Business*, enunciated a simple but very wise management principle which has been part of my working philosophy ever since I read it. He said:

Every successful business is based on a *philosophy* which represents its reason for being. Out of this philosophy its *principles* are developed. Out of these principles its *policies* are evolved. To serve these policies, *methods* are provided.

The basic *philosophy* of a business should be sacrosanct, once it has been proved sound. Nothing short of an action of the Board of Directors should change its *principles*. Its *policies* should be revised to fit changing times and needs, albeit only after prudent deliberation. As for its *methods*, they should be changed or discarded whenever they become obsolete or better ones can be worked out.

Policies, in particular, must be the top man's constant concern, for it is largely its policies which keep a company competitive—or fail to. And he must be watchful that they never become too sacred to be challenged, which would stifle the business.

To avoid that, the chief executive will do well to ask himself from time to time: Is this or that policy still sound? Or are we hiding behind it to save ourselves hard thinking, or to postpone making a difficult decision?

BANISHING "SACRED COWS" AND GREMLINS

He should employ a management meeting every now and then to involve all his key people in thinking about their responsibility not to permit *any* company policy to become a "sacred cow." One of the most successful such meetings we ever had was one entirely devoted to questioning "sacred cows" —with no holds barred. As a result, we made several constructive policy revisions.

"Sacred cows" reminds me to sound a warning to new chief executives about, of all things, reincarnation. As he assumes his new office, the head man ought to reflect on how many times on his way to the top he and contemporaries in management were slowed down by a busy little gremlin who went by his predecessor's first name, followed by the word "thinks."

If the predecessor's given name, for example, was Throckmorton, the gremlin's name was "Throckmorton Thinks." And he was all over the place, involving himself in just about everything that went on throughout the company management. He was invisible, and he wasn't on the payroll, nor did he have any status. He was sort of an echo, frequently heard but never seen, but he wielded a tremendous amount of influence. Whenever a problem arose, or an opinion was asked, or a decision was needed, "Throckmorton Thinks" got into the act.

It took a year or so for me to realize that Mr. Whatever-his-first-name-is Thinks has more lives than a cat. When I recognized that this elusive little fellow had been reincarnated as "Charlie Thinks," I decided I could not ignore such an influential gremlin, that I should at least *try* to catch him.

My talk at a management meeting was devoted to this task. I frankly told my key people that I had done what they do when they want to know what's going on under the surface. I had tuned in on the grapevine, for I had found that the trusty grapevine works *up*, as well as *down*, and *sidewise*. I told them I had heard plenty—"Charlie Thinks this—and that—and this—and that—and this—and that."

I cited a great many potentially disruptive "Charlie Thinks" examples which had no basis in fact whatsoever. Then I spelled out meticulously what Charlie really *did* think on 16 specific subjects. The point of the whole talk, of course, was to urge these very important management people never to let what "Charlie Thinks" stop them from thinking for themselves. I *think* it worked.

In planning a management meeting, I have found it is extremely effective to lodge in the limited number attending the firm responsibility for later conveying down the line what takes place in the meeting. Copies of top officers' talks are *not* made available, but taking voluminous notes is encouraged. Thus the manager-level attendee returns to his staff with more than merely dull pieces of paper to pass around perfunctorily—and then, for the most part, to gather dust. Part of his job is to tell his people in his own words what was said at the meeting, and interpret the application to his particular operations. If he can get by with merely passing out copies of the speeches, he won't accomplish the same good result.

By designating these as "invitation meetings" rather than management meetings, you can plan them around specific subjects or problems and invite those—and only those—members of the management concerned with the particular subject. Thus the discussions can be more sharply focused, and those in management not invited because they are not involved this time fully understand. Flexibility such as this is not as easy in a decentralized company, whose operating divisional managements are scattered geographically as my company's were for several years. Now, instead of having our division headquarters' staffs located at each division's main processing plant, we have moved all the domestic management groups into our corporate headquarters in White Plains, New York.

DECENTRALIZATION—IN SUBURBIA

This has proven to have many advantages. Perhaps the most important is the greater degree of easy mobility of people, even at high levels, which the company can now maintain. Promotions, and even lateral transfers for the gaining of broader experience, are facilitated when moving a manager from one division to another. It isn't necessary for the man to move his family from one section of the country to another; he merely moves to a different office in one of the headquarters buildings. And you can be sure this minimizing of the uprooting of families is appreciated by managers' wives. They relish the idea of their youngsters being able to stay in the same school and keep their friends.

From the management point of view, this arrangement—with the divisions still autonomously profit-responsible yet closer to the influence of corporate leadership—facilitates the total operation. Each division can concentrate on its own products and business. At the same time, on a daily basis an interdivisional and corporate-divisional exchange of ideas and approaches to problem-solving goes on continuously in scheduled meetings and informally around the lunch table. In our unique so-called campus setting in Westchester, corporate management thus has an everyday opportunity to observe all levels of divisional management.

I'm often asked how I feel—11 years after the fact—about our move from the city to the suburbs. The box score comes out strongly and clearly on the plus side. The shoulder rubbing I've just mentioned is one of the greatest plusses. A few more may be of interest.

It is easier to build and maintain a close family spirit in a spacious, campus-like setting than in a city skyscraper. Our productivity has risen, as has the calibre of the people we attract. There are fewer applicants but they screen much higher on the average. In general, people tend to stay with us longer, so our turnover rate is lower. Individualized transportation is so much the way of life today that the certainty of a parking place on the premises of employment has become a major, albeit unspecified, fringe benefit. So is a good lunch at a low price.

The thorough, even painstaking, way our headquarters move to the suburbs was planned and executed gave us both a fine foundation and good start—and doubtless is largely responsible for the success which the move has enjoyed. And all this I can say without immodesty, for it was the administration preceding my own which managed the years-long preparation for an implementation of the move to White Plains. The key element was the keep-employees-informed policy under which all General Foods people were given a sense of participation in this major corporate decision.

PROFITS—FROM A FEELING OF BELONGING

Indeed, this policy has served the company well over the years. Right now, we are nearing the dedication of a new plant at Dover, Delaware, which consolidates the production of four outmoded operations in the East. It is most gratifying that the closing of these plants has been accomplished with a minimum of misunderstanding and hard feelings in the communities, and that this major move is being used as a case history in a book to be distributed by the American Management Association.

More than anyone else, a chief executive should know the value of spreading the spirit and feeling of belonging. And this makes it incumbent upon him not only to provide appropriate monetary incentives for his people, but also to initiate and extend all down the line the concept that the people who work for *his* company are investing their business lives as truly as stockholders are investing their money. It is a basic philosophical fact that people with a sense of investing themselves, and who know that their management regards them as investors of their business careers, will produce better products, render better customer service, and give fuller measure of value to the public than people who are merely working to earn a living.

57

Such contributions as the above add to the greater profitability of the company. And that, of course, is "the name of the game." That is the chief executive's first basic responsibility—to increase profitability and build a firm foundation for future growth. Creating constructive attitudes among employees will help him do this and is well worth the time it takes.

His people's attitudes, the chief executive usually finds, are reflected in the degree of receptivity they show to the motivating or—to use a distasteful word—"needling" he must do. They will be responsive, for example, when he finds it necessary to admonish the management against being lulled by current success and warns against coasting just because things are going so well.

Keeping the company in momentum, once he gets it there, is one of the toughest jobs of the chief executive. Not only he, but all of his key people, need to recall their high school physics—that it takes less energy to keep a body in momentum than it does to get it in momentum in the first place. And the chief executive is the one who periodically must recall this principle to the minds of his organization.

Without such guidance, some management people will find being in momentum a thoroughly relaxed and enjoyable sensation. They get the notion that momentum alone will carry the company sufficiently, whereas we all know it must be constantly reactivated and stepped up or it dies down—fast.

Everyone in the company can get into the greater momentum act. Every member of the management team can contribute to the momentum of the business through developments appropriate to his or her particular area of responsibility. The marketing man can make his contribution through thinking up new ways to sell more of a particular product. The office services man can make his contribution through thinking up a more efficient or less expensive way to provide a housekeeping service. The staff man in engineering can make his contribution by suggesting a better way to do a production job.

GENERATING THE WILL TO WORK

All this may seem obvious, but people do need to be reminded. They also need to be reminded of something not as obvious: that unless each gives first attention to the potential in his own backyard —in his own individual job responsibility—no one else is going to make up for his failure, even if he is applying his mind to something he thinks could result in a more dramatic contribution to the business.

Primary application to one's responsibility demands self-discipline. Far pastures always look greener. Also, familiarity breeds contempt, and a man understandably can get to thinking that he is in a prosaic, relatively dull job, which won't yield even to the most imaginative thinking.

Here, a concomitant obligation of the chief executive comes into play. It isn't enough for him to enunciate the theory that if everyone did a bang-up job in the area of his own responsibility the company would be in clover. He must make it very clear that it is his intention that the individual who *does* a bang-up job in his particular field need not worry about otherwise having to attract attention to himself. He must see to it that the company's promotion policy—from himself on down—demonstrates consistently that such a man is given an early opportunity in a broader field.

For if the company is to keep growing, its people must grow. But people are not all alike in their attitude toward the company. There are those who want to "succeed without really trying," and even some who don't really care much about succeeding at all. Only now is this nation beginning to come to grips with the problem such people represent. There are more of them in our total society than it is comfortable to contemplate.

This was brought home to me forcefully in a talk I heard Secretary of Labor Willard Wirtz make about the school drop-outs, many of whom become and remain chronically unemployed. The Secretary said that studies of households caught in what sociologists call the "cycle of poverty" indicate that the will to learn, later followed by the will to work, is developed in children as early as age three to six. This strongly suggests that, as a nation, in our quest for a sound society, we may well have to change our primary focus on the problem of drop-outs and unemployment and start at the family environment stage, rather than with the school and employment office.

In his own never-ending quest for people who *do* have the will to work, who *are* capable of growing and who thus help the company grow, the chief executive is looking for the relatively rare man who will get completely involved. The man he wants is the kind willing to "marry" the company—one who wouldn't dream of "divorcing" it. Usually, such a man has a wife, but he manages to keep peace with this third member of the triangle, the little lady at home, while meeting fully his responsibilities first to the business and second to his career.

Accompanying the will to work and to become wholly involved with his job, there must be whole-hearted willingness really to accept personal responsibility, and particularly the *individual* responsibility to make decisions.

THE ART OF DECISION-MAKING

Secretary of State Dean Rusk, in a meeting I attended, spoke of the way the State Department must get things done. Down the line, said he, each man "makes those decisions which lay within the horizons of his own responsibility." In a business organization, it is a ceaseless task to imbue people with this concept—that each must, indeed, "make those decisions within the horizons of his own responsibility," even if these decisions may be only to seek approval further up the line.

In business, hard and frequently important decisions have to be made daily. Right decisions build profits and produce growth. Wrong ones slow you down. They concern such vital problems as whether or not to build or expand a plant; to pursue a given major program of research and development; to launch a big new product; and even whether or not to withdraw from the marketplace—*now*—a long-run apparently insufficiently profitable new product. Because profits can be *conserved* by knowing when to quit.

To my mind, decision-making is an art—not a science. It is a serious error even to think of decision-making as a science. Such thinking envisions a foolproof formula of some kind that will guarantee a high batting average of right decisions.

There is no way to insure a good decision. We can do no better than to delineate all the various alternatives, assess the advantages and disadvantages of each, and decide on the one we think will work best.

63

The factor of judgment in effective decision-making cannot be overrated or supplanted. Scientific data, research, computers, and market tests are a welcome supplement to judgment. They can supply, much better than hunch or opinion, the intelligence needed for decision-making, but they cannot supply the required judgment.

One more point about decision-making should be stressed. This has to do with the necessity for having the courage to admit when a wrong decision has been made and to take early steps to correct it. When my company introduces a new product, we back it from the start with all the ingenuity and resources at our command. But when our judgment tells us it is failing to measure up in terms of profitability, we back off from it as soon as we can. It is a prime responsibility of good management, once it finds that it is barking up the wrong tree, to curtail losses as much as possible—losses of money, losses of valuable people's valuable time, and losses of other corporate resources.

In its zeal to develop new products, a company should not overlook the real possibilities in the further development of some of its existing products

64

which might be improved just enough in quality or novelty or convenience to make them more satisfying and more highly marketable.

In the food business, as a matter of fact, it can become a very costly proposition to reach too far out for products if they call for changes in basic eating habits. The American people change basic tastes very slowly. By the same token, in expanding abroad, the tastes of each *country* must be fully recognized. It just doesn't do to assume that a country's food habits can be changed by products which have won high popularity in the United States.

I have a true story to illustrate this point. Wally Erskine, one of our Canadian subsidiary executives, told it to me. While on Air Force leave in London during World War II, he took a busman's holiday and browsed through a grocery store to see how our British cousins conducted their business. What struck him most was a display of Maxwell House ground coffee in little quarter-pound cans.

When a woman plucked one off the shelf, Wally —who was used to one, two or even three-pound cans of coffee—just couldn't refrain from asking her about the practicality of buying in such a small quantity.

"How long can such a little can last?" was his question.

"Oh, a good long while," the shopper replied. "You see, my 'Arry is awful hard to get up in the morning. So first thing every morning I boil a pot of water and drop just a half teaspoon of this coffee in it. Pretty soon the aroma is all over our flat and gets to 'Arry. He yawns, stretches and says: 'M-m-m-m . . . don't that smell good. Let's get up and brew a pot of tea.' "

DEVELOPMENT BENEFITS FROM SCROUNGING

Even in our own country, the realistic approach to development of grocery products is to strive for improved items which are identified with existing basic consumer tastes or appetites. Worthwhile scientific discoveries or breakthroughs are rare indeed in our business, and then usually require long-time effort and large investment to translate into eventual public desires, which result in profits.

How development—of products and hence of a company—may be accelerated by keeping a sharp lookout for fairly obvious opportunities is illustrated by a personal experience. Seven years ago, I spent a day in St. Paul with some of the officers of Minnesota Mining & Manufacturing, a company for whose enterprise and business sagacity I have always had profound respect. I brought back with me a word which I was told is the basis of much of 3M's success.

This word is *scrounging*. It is a picturesque English slang word which the dictionary defines sketchily as meaning "to pilfer, to take for one's own." But as used at 3M (and I might add by my company since my visit), it could be defined broadly as the way to uncover internal profits by digging in new fields; by adapting and applying discoveries and techniques from other industries; by searching in unlikely places.

Over the past seven years, I have observed that every function, every product, every resource, every facility of a business is capable of development by the scrounging method to contribute to increased profits. An important opportunity to scrounge lies in adapting ideas or discoveries made in other product areas. We have even scrounged a whole new successful product—Dream Whip Whipped Topping Mix—out of a search for a way to keep fat homogenized in cake mixes.

Another example of scrounging for sizeable profits was in the area of fuller utilization of a single sheet of paper. We simply changed the product-envelope of Kool-Aid from a center-seam to a side-seam seal, and one-fifth more envelopes were produced from the same size sheet.

Scrounging can indeed be profitable, and the dollars it yields are just as acceptable to stockholders as any derived from any other aspect of a company's development program. The important point is that scrounging be given the high place it deserves in the development program.

The ascendancy of research and development in American business in recent years has been phenomenal. Of all the words that I have heard and read on this subject, I like best a brief paragraph from the annual report of the Radio Corporation of America a few years ago. "Research, in its simplified definition, is the distance between the problem and the answer. The challenge facing us all is to continue to reduce that distance."

Closing the gap between problem and answer underscores the element of time. Time is of the utmost importance, particularly in my $82 billion food industry, where some 8,000 items now compete on grocery shelves that held only 1,500 fifteen years ago, and where hard-won consumer franchises have to be reconfirmed every single day in the myriad supermarkets across the nation.

A GOOD QUESTION: HOW SOON?

Seven years ago we devoted an entire management meeting to trying to open our key people's minds to the realization that all of us needed to put extra emphasis on the element of time in accelerating the company's development program. Here is how it happened, in the words I used in talking to my team—for I find I can't improve on the way I said it then.

> You have heard of the seven-year itch. Well, I have a bad case of seven-year itch—an itch to develop this business to the full extent I believe it *can* be developed, before I turn in my uniform.
>
> The key to progress in a great cooperative program of development can be summed up in a two-word question: *How soon?*

How *soon* can we start on this or that plan or project?

How *soon* can you have samples of the product?

How *soon* can you have the figures?

How *soon* can you get into production?

How *soon* can you make the necessary contact?

How *soon* can the test marketing be done?

How *soon* can the advertising get into print or on the air?

How *soon* can you take the necessary trip?

How *soon* can the promotion plans be ready?

How *soon* can you have the answer?

From now on you are going to hear that question a lot, starting from my office and filtering down through every division and department— *How soon? How soon? How soon?*

Call it 'How Soon? Management' if you will. With increasingly determined—and able—compeition crowding in on us from every side, we haven't time to take our time.

At the same meeting where I made this effort to induce a sense of urgency, I felt it was appropriate to put forward an accompanying concept I have long held on the process of thinking.

There are, it has always seemed to me, three steps to the thinking process. The first is to *think about* an idea, plan, or project. Sometimes we think *about* things for years without getting any benefit from the mental energy expended. Thus, *thinking about* is often a procrastinating form of thinking.

The second step is *to think into* an idea, plan, or project. This entails bringing to bear on the problem experience, analytical ability, imagination, inventiveness, resourcefulness.

The third—and I think most important—step is *to think through*. This involves enlisting the best judgment that can be mustered on every phase and facet of the idea, plan, or proposal. This three-step process faces realities, assays the possibilities of success or failure, objectively canvasses the potentials, and then organizes the proposed plan or project so carefully that its success is far better assured.

Thinking through is well exemplified by Abraham Lincoln's reported method of thinking: to bound an idea on the east, west, north and south before adopting or rejecting it. Too often, under the pressures of our business day, we bound an idea on three sides but overlook the fourth—which may be its most exposed and vulnerable side.

This thinking-through process will prevent rushing into ventures which otherwise might prove to be ill-considered. It can become a habit, the *modus operandi* of a business organization, and should be employed before starting anything new, changing anything, or abolishing anything.

Until we have *thought through*, it is foolhardy to act. But that doesn't mean that we have to dawdle or postpone or stall or procrastinate. Nor does it interfere with "How Soon?" management. Rather, it poses the question: How soon can I possibly *think through* whatever it is I am considering doing?

Assuming that, after thinking *through* we decide to go ahead, then all of the detailed "How Soon?" questions come into play. From then on it is a matter of maintaining unremitting pressure in the pleasantest firm fashion of which you are capable.

Two days after the "How Soon?" management meeting, one executive brought me a small framed sign he had made and placed it on my desk so no visitor could miss it. It read simply: "How Soon?" Next thing I knew, similar signs sprouted on desks and walls all over our buildings, and before long they were also in the field. When my associates nicknamed me "How Soon?" Mortimer, I was downright pleased that my communication of the necessary sense of urgency had been effective.

Of course, the chief executive cannot always have the unmatchable benefits of face-to-face communication. And so it will pay him—and the company —for him to give personal painstaking attention to his and other important written as well as oral communications. He can make sure that bulletins, written policies, employee and customer publications, all really communicate—really say the right things in the right way to create the right effect.

THE PROFITABILITY IN POOLING

Communications constitute an indispensable weapon in the chief executive's arsenal as he strives perennially to motivate his organization toward the purposeful pursuit of profits and growth. He needs to train this high-calibred instrument on developing in his people a unified spirit of concern for the success of the entire enterprise so that even as each individual gives primary attention to the specific job he has in hand he also applies his abilities and experience for the benefit of the *whole business*.

There is a tendency for the organization chart, with each man's name in its own little box, to put a wall around each executive position. It is very easy for an executive so boxed in to adopt the attitude of

"You keep out of my domain, and I'll keep out of yours." The result is too little cross-fertilization of ideas and experience, to the detriment of the business in its unified pursuit of profits and growth.

There is no magic preventative for this organization malady. But there is a concept which I have earnestly tried to promote. Let me share with you these brief paragraphs I used to crystallize this concept to our management group:

There is profit-and-growth magic in the principle of *pooling*. Our large decentralized organization—with its broadly experienced staff services and its several operating divisions, each with a valuable accumulation of know-how—represents a great *pool* of ability, experience and creativeness. While each of us is called upon to make a comparatively small contribution *to* the pool, we can all draw on the *whole pool*. Each man will do well to ask himself two questions—not just once, but frequently:

1. Am I availing myself of all the useful help I can get from others in the company?

2. Am I doing everything I can to strengthen the whole company, while I do a building job in my own division or department?

The key to each division's or department's success and growth is the success and growth of the corporation; the key to the corporation's success and growth is the *pooled* success and growth of all its components.

This, to me, is one of the real challenges confronting the chief executive: To enlist—and purposefully utilize—*all* of the experience, *all* of the talents and abilities of his people and rev up his organization for the more purposeful pursuit of profits and growth.

There can be no greater challenge to any chief executive. And there can be no greater motivation for a younger man on the way up who aspires some day to that exalted title and sobering responsibility. Building a good organization—fielding a winning team—is an experience that is as rewarding as it is requiring, and as requiring as it is rewarding.

3

THE BIFOCAL APPROACH
TO PROFITS AND GROWTH

*"Minding today's store" isn't enough—
the chief executive must concern himself
with the climate in which business operates.*

The concept of adopting a bifocal approach to profits and growth was contributed—in a way—by Benjamin Franklin, a very practical and perceptive man, as illustrated by this paragraph from *Benjamin Franklin's Own Story*, written by Nathan G. Goodman and published by the University of Pennsylvania Press:

> The weak and strained eyes of Franklin saw much more than the strong eyes of most men. As they grew steadily weaker, he employed two pairs of spectacles, and it was his custom to carry reading glasses in his coat pocket. One day, however, as Franklin walked in the Market House his friends noticed he was wearing a singularly strange-looking pair of spectacles. They were strange, perhaps, but they were practical. He had been annoyed at the nuisance of carrying the extra pair, and so he had solved the problem by grinding the first pair of bifocals.

Bifocal spectacles were one of Benjamin Franklin's most practical contributions to mankind. But the bifocal idea is not limited to *physical* vision. We can be bifocal in a much broader sense. As applied to the pursuit of profits and growth for his company, the chief executive will of necessity adopt the bifocal approach as a daily—almost hourly—means for the successful administration of his business.

He is bound to have plenty of immediate problems, which he must look at close up. These are his near-vision responsibilities, involving the day-to-day carry-on of the business.

But quite as importantly, he must keep the business on a profitable course, long range. That is his distant-vision responsibility and one he cannot delegate. Everything he is doing today—each decision he makes in connection with his immediate problems—has an influence on that future; just as every long-range plan he makes affects in some measure what he ought to be doing today.

When he is looking at a plan or problem close up, he can glance up quickly and look through the distance lenses of his bifocals and ask himself how today's plan or decision will affect the business two, three, five years hence. Or, when he is engaged in future planning—whether it is in connection with a basic change in organization, a new plant, a long-range financing program, a new line of products, a new service, or whatever—it is important that he glance down from time to time. That way he can view the project through the near-view lenses, to see how it will affect immediate profits and the near-term welfare of the business.

In short, there is most surely a *tomorrow* aspect to almost every plan or decision we make *today*; and there is a *today* aspect to every plan we are making for *tomorrow*. Hence the need for a bifocal look at just about everything we do, every day.

ASSESSING THE BUSINESS BIFOCALLY

The bifocal principle can profitably be applied to assessing the executive personnel of the organization. The chief executive should look at each man bifocally, asking himself such questions as:

What should I be doing *now* to have Mr. A. ready for tomorrow's much heavier responsibilities that I see developing in his area?

Is Mr. B., who seems to have such genius for long-range planning, sufficiently conscious of the need for *immediate* progress and profits?

Especially in his quest for the man to succeed him in the top job when he retires, the chief executive should look at performance bifocally. Is the man who appears to be the most likely prospect today capable of developing appropriately over the long pull?

As already stated, the search is for a man who will "marry" the company. The rare quality wanted is that unique motivating force which McGeorge Bundy has so aptly called "the simple, natural, almost unexaminable human desire to do something really well." And when, if ever, he finds such a man, the chief executive will do well to follow the advice in the song from *South Pacific*. He should "never let him go."

A bifocal approach will help the chief executive see people not only in the light of their present performances but also keep an eye on their various potentials for development. It will help him establish remuneration programs which not only pay well on a month-by-month basis, but also provide longer-range monetary incentives such as deferred payment bonuses and stock options.

There are many broader questions about the

business which the chief executive will ask himself
if he adopts the bifocal approach. For example, he
will raise such questions as:

What can we do to make our customers want to
do more business with us, in preference to our
competitors, not only this year but also two years,
five years, or even ten years from now?

Earlier, I touched on the fact that in my company we did ask precisely this question. One important part of the answer we came up with was the
planning and building of a nationwide network of
20 market-centered sales and distribution centers,
which now enable us to fill customers' orders more
promptly and dependably. With our warehouses located near them and capable of guaranteeing delivery on the day they need the merchandise, customers can do as much or more business with
smaller inventories of our products. This results in
faster turnover and greater profit for them.

As a matter of fact, most of our customers actually do business on our money, for they can order
and get a delivery every seven days, while our credit
terms are two per cent, ten days. This minimizing

of cash tied up in inventory of our products gives our customers a very sound reason for wanting to do more business with us, just as we foresaw 10 years ago when we looked soberly through the upper part of our bifocals at the necessarily large capital investment to build the network of distribution centers.

"MINDING THE STORE" IS NOT ENOUGH

So far I have dealt with using the bifocal approach *within* the business. But there is another way in which the chief executive needs to be bifocal. He must, of course, concentrate most of his attention on the welfare of his own business, but from time to time he should observe through the upper part of his bifocals what is going on outside —the influences in his industry, and even more importantly, those in his community and state and throughout the nation which bear on the profits and growth of his business and all business.

It is no longer enough merely to "mind the store" well. Today's businessman must also keep an eye on and seek ways to improve the neighborhood in which he does business. In other words, he has obligations to society and a responsibility for helping to preserve our private enterprise system.

He must combine enlightened self-interest with serving the public interest. For there is a public interest in almost everything a business does today or hopes to do tomorrow. For what is going on outside the business area—locally, nationally, and even internationally—in some measure directly or indirectly affects all private business.

Executives should find a way to steal some of that precious element of time away from "minding the store" to use it for the purpose of advancing the interests of their total industry and for improving the over-all business climate. They need to help provide better understanding in America about the indispensable role business has in enhancing the strength of our country's economy.

The voice of the thoughtful businessman is being listened to today—and his counsel sought, both by our public servants in government and by the public in general. This is most encouraging. The opportunity for bifocal viewing of business's partnership relations with government in the strengthening of national economy has never been better, nor more vitally needed.

World conditions demand that we who administer businesses develop a sense of history as it is being made in our time and a keen awareness that all of us have responsibilities which transcend the need merely to run our own businesses well. In addition to serving the consumers of our products efficiently, we need from time to time to review our operations in terms of the national interest. For today our country has an aggressive and increasingly formidable competitor for world influence—the people of Russia. And I use the expression—people of Russia—intentionally.

Ever since I visited Russia briefly in 1959, I have had a disturbing feeling that the key factor in Russia's transformation from a backward nation to its present competitive status is the ability and willingness of her *people* to identify themselves and their individual goals with their country's economic aims and objectives—about which too many of our people seem to be apathetic.

I am by no means the first to say this—and I fervently hope I won't be the last, for it needs saying over and over again—but the time is long past due for all of us to recognize the indispensability of this kind of dedication in the world in which we are living today.

A while back Malcolm Muir, the late editor-in-chief of *Newsweek*, had this to say about the Russians' economic progress: "Behind it all, there is a sense of purpose or urgency, and a crusading spirit which is a profound challenge to all Americans."

In this challenge, business has an enormous stake. It also has an inescapable responsibility—the responsibility of providing leadership for promoting the ability and willingness of our people to identify themselves and their individual goals closely with our country's national aims and objectives.

BUSINESS CAN PROMOTE "PEACEFUL COEXISTENCE"

The need for producing such a healthy spirit among Americans comes crystal clear to me when, every so often, I indulge in an interesting mental exercise. I pretend, as I read the morning newspaper, that I am a citizen of one of the many countries which both the Communists and the United States are wooing. Try it some day. I promise an enlightening experience—and a frightening one.

From what you read in the paper, you get the distinct impression that this nation is divided into three major warring camps. There is one called Business (with a capital B); another called Labor (with a capital L); and a third labeled Government (with a capital G). They seem to have little or nothing in common. And each seems to be claiming all the credit for everything that is good about our American way of life. There is scarcely an inkling that none of the three could possibly exist without the other two.

By putting yourself mentally in the place of a citizen in an emerging nation, someone who is trying to decide which system to vote for his country to follow in order to improve his own bare subsistence level, I am afraid you would soon get this impression: that even though the United States is a land of plenty, its people are constantly erecting selfish barriers to interfere with their country's optimum growth through maximum efficiency.

Right here at home, among all Americans, there

is need for broader and deeper understanding that the "coexistence," practiced in our international relations, should not be confined to a nation-to-nation basis. Business has a responsibility to help make it clear that our nation's well-being, to say nothing of our relationships with the rest of the world, depends in large measure upon our varied interest groups being able to practice "peaceful coexistence" on the domestic front.

I feel sure business could provide better leadership by recognizing what politicians know instinctively—that the way to gain support is not by being negative, or defensive, or timid, but by being positive, creative, and constructive; by being *for* what is good for people; by being *for* what people want, and then sincerely trying to help them get it.

Businessmen pride themselves on their skill in promoting goods and services. Should they not put this experience and ability—in *positive* fashion— behind the promotion of sound ideas for "peaceful coexistence" of all segments of our society which would strengthen the vitality of our country?

More businessmen need to come forward with some very plain talk to clarify the relationships between the various parts of our economic life. They need to make it clearer that business is the great generator which helps all the elements of our national life to perform as well as they do.

This is a business country. Business is what makes the mare go in these United States. If altogether too many Americans do not understand this —and seemingly they do not—who has a greater responsibility than corporate executives for making known these basic facts:

- Two out of three of our nation's 73 million wage earners are employed by business and industry.
- Millions of labor union members wouldn't be carrying home substantial weekly pay checks if it weren't for business.
- Jobs—productive employment—can be provided only by successful, growing businesses.
- Poverty can be lessened only in a country where business and profits are good, because profitable businesses generate most of the Federal and state taxes used in combating these social and economic ills.

The positioning of business as a key factor in American life—not only one's own business but Business with a capital B—is part of every chief executive's responsibility. And for my part, operating in the grocery industry, I like to deal in simple concepts when making a speech or writing an article on the subject. "Grocery store economics" might be a fitting characterization of my style.

One of the most effective word-pictures I have hit upon is the concept of a three-way mirror of good citizenship in which our country's over-all well-being is reflected. I originally presented the concept at my company's stockholders' meeting in 1962 in these words:

> Each of us plays three roles in our economy, as reflected in the good-citizenship mirror.
>
> First of all, everyone sees himself as a consumer. That's obvious from a straight-ahead look in the citizenship mirror. Then, by looking simultaneously in one of the mirror's side panels, some 73 million of us who are employed can see ourselves not only as consumers but also as producers or earners. Of these, more than 16½ million are members of labor unions.

In the mirror's other side panel, about 120 million of us are reflected. These are all the investors, thanks to the savings made possible by our American abundance which yields discretionary income —money above and beyond what we need just to live. More than a hundred million of us are indirect investors through a variety of financial institutions such as mutual savings banks, insurance companies, pension funds, and so on. Sixteen and a half million adults—very close to the total number belonging to unions—are stockholders in American corporations.

Those who limit their vision to any one of the three panels of the citizenship mirror see only a pocketbook issue. And this accounts for the great apathy toward the infinitely more important overall issues—the national interest issues having to do with our very economic survival.

The consumer is primarily interested in prices. He lives *by* them.

To the worker, wages are all-important. He lives *on* them.

The investor looks to profits. He lives *because of* them.

Business must live *with*, *on* and *by* all three— prices, wages and profits. . . . Profits are vital to investment, and we must invest before we can produce and we must produce before we can consume.

Unhappily, I fear businessmen have contributed to the misunderstanding of the function of profits by using language in published statements which, while familiar vernacular to us, has confusing or unfortunate connotations to the general public.

For example, the term "retained earnings" doubtless is perpetuating the erroneous notion that the profits of a business are something "left over" and hoarded away in a vault. Accountants use this term to identify profits not paid out in dividends to investors, but a far better public-opinion phrase would be "money available for growth." Businessmen know that is exactly what it is. But Mr. and Mrs. Average Citizen do not.

PUBLIC UNDERSTANDING NEEDED FOR ECONOMIC GROWTH

It is very clear to me that American business leaders—and business teachers—share the responsibility of helping make the indispensability of business profits "come alive" to the man in the street and the woman in the kitchen. What could be more important to our national welfare than to change public opinion to a positive one about the essentiality of healthy profits to a burgeoning economy?

We need to get over these four simple economic facts:

1. When American business hurts, so does the whole American economy.

2. When there aren't enough profits, there isn't enough investment, and this affects the number of jobs.

3. That the number of jobs and the rate of profits are inseparably connected.

4. That unless the millions of business investors can see at least the *prospect* of a good profit, they will curtail their venture investments and thus the faster rising economic growth we need to strengthen us as a nation cannot and will not be attained.

This clarification of the nature and function of profits is essential if we are to remove still another barrier to growth—the hostility to bigness in business.

In any business which sells to the consuming public, the public itself is responsible for that enterprise becoming bigger. If the business serves its public acceptably, and at a profit, it can hardly keep from growing. Its customers will, in fact, insist on making it grow—and continue to grow—by giving it more of their patronage, year after year.

This is true even of the smallest business. The man who opens a four-stool, one-table, hole-in-the-wall lunchroom and really satisfies his customers, and does so *at a profit*, will have to knock down the wall between his place and the vacant shop next door before too long. Else his satisfied customers will turn into *dissatisfied* customers and take their patronage elsewhere because he doesn't have the larger capacity to serve all of them what they want, when they want it.

My personal philosophy of profit-making is summed up in this simple definition: If you do a job of serving the public intelligently and acceptably, profits and growth will ensue as naturally as day follows night.

Those who persistently impute badness to bigness would do well to remember that a business cannot grow big without becoming a big customer for labor; a big customer for raw materials; a big customer for tools, machinery, bricks and mortar; a big customer for office equipment and supplies; a big customer for engineering, construction, transportation, communication, scientific research, advertising, insurance, financing, and scores of other services—all of which provide jobs for workers on a big scale in a wide variety of crafts, skills and professions.

Bigness is the result of growth. Growth is a law of nature. To try to controvert this law is unnatural. Thus, hostility toward bigness, per se, can be self-defeating. For, in trying to circumvent nature's law, we could wind up stifling the great force for good which much of bigness has proved itself to be in our economy and in improving our standard of living.

THE "MIDDLEMAN" IS NO VILLAIN

A third sadly misunderstood important facet of our economy—besides the function of profits and of bigness—is what has come to be called "the middleman." Here, again, public apathy and hostility undermine the very rising standard of living for which we are striving by beclouding the way in which our system creates jobs for farm workers, transportation employees, production workers, salesmen, advertising practitioners, retail clerks, to mention only some of the categories of employment along the road to market.

These workers really are "the middleman." If more people saw them in that light, perhaps the word "middleman" would no longer carry the connotation of "all take and no give" which has stigmatized it for centuries. Since earliest civilizations, a middleman has been portrayed as one who buys cheap and sells dear, contributing nothing to the value of the goods in the process. That *may* have been true, way back. But today the villain the critics of our system pursue is no villain at all.

In our urbanized, industrialized society, the middlemen—in the food industry, for example—are all the people who take raw food from the farm or other place of origin and then make it possible and desirable for people to eat it. Milk in a pail at a farmer's gate is worth nothing to the nine out of ten Americans who live off the farm. Consumers can't possibly all drive out and get their daily quart. The only way milk takes on value is through its availability when and where the consumer can conveniently get it. Consumers simply won't pay for wheat in the barn, peas on the vine, and raw hamburger on the hoof.

Along the job-creating road to market, the "middleman" encompasses all the vast activity that goes on from farm gate to check-out counter. This has built and sustained the nation's market for processed farm products. And this adds value after value—at a reasonable cost—every step of the way.

It is disturbing—and ironical—that so many in all walks of life in this country who benefit from our marketplace and the values it brings continue to carp and criticize the American system. Business executives never cease to wonder at the misunderstanding and hostility which persist toward the freedom of enterprise which is so important to our national prosperity and progress.

I cannot refrain from noting here that apathy, and even antipathy, extend all too frequently into the academic fraternity. Educators prize academic freedom as highly as businessmen treasure freedom of enterprise. And that is all to the good.

But in exercising the freedom of thought and expression, there is a definite risk of replacing belief with non-belief, of eroding the foundations of public faith in those institutions which we most need to preserve. There is much to be gained from criticism of the existing order of things by the intellectual—provided that the criticism is constructive. Much of the destructive criticism of the profit system and of bigness in business comes from some of our outstandingly respected academicians, and this I find very discouraging.

It reminds me of a story Edward R. Murrow used to tell about the two cowboys making camp on the Western prairie, after spending a hard day rounding up the last meager herd of the vanishing American buffalo which were grazing nearby. One cowboy said: "I don't understand all this concern about preserving those critters. Every one of them is a filthy dirty mangy beast. If I had my way I'd shoot them all and wipe out the breed." Whereupon one bull buffalo muttered to the other: "Partner, in our last home on the range, I think I have finally heard a discouraging word."

FREE ENTERPRISE MUST BE SOLD IN SCHOOL

The educators—particularly those who ride herd on business school students—need to be sure that their criticism of our economic system is constructive. They need to be extraordinarily concerned with the way they go about implanting points of view in the minds of young people, many of whom soon will be playing important roles in our free enterprise economy.

The function of criticism is to sharpen the intellect, not to substitute one bias for another, or to tear down while offering nothing of value in replacement. I know I am not alone among businessmen who are concerned about the extent to which cynicism has wormed its way into our national attitude.

Tearing down has always been easier then building up. As a grandfather 13 times over, I am, like all grandfathers, indulgent of my young grandchildren —but also fascinated by their destructive instincts and their joy in tearing down. If you have ever helped a three-year-old build a tower of blocks, you know that he takes far more delight in leveling the tower with one sweep of his hand or foot than he ever displays in building it.

But in our institutions of higher learning we are not dealing with very young children. It is here, with our budding citizens, that educators need to score the points which are the very hope of our society for the future: that to build, rather than to tear down, is the measure of man's maturity, and that the progress of mankind is built upon positive faith and affirmative action. It is here that we have an obligation to develop the abiding faith in the American system which will alter the skeptical attitudes so many of our young people today hold toward both business and education.

If this sounds too much like a businessman's sermon, let me take cover by invoking the words of an eminent educator—one of America's self-styled "intellectuals," Professor George J. Stigler of the University of Chicago's Graduate School of Business, published in a most refreshing article last summer. It was titled "The Intellectual and the Marketplace," and appeared in a publication of Washington University at St. Louis.

One might logically expect, Professor Stigler wrote, that the intellectual would be more kindly disposed toward the private enterprise system because intellectuals, by and large, have elevated tastes; they like to eat, dress and live well, and especially to travel. And since intellectuals are not inexpensive,

Professor Stigler notes that until the rise of the modern enterprise system, no society could afford many of them. He wrote: "As a wild guess, the full-time intellectuals numbered 200 in Athens in the extraordinary age of Pericles, or about one for every 1,500 of population . . . Today, there are at least one million in the United States, or one for each 200 of population."

Professor Stigler makes the point that at least four out of five intellectuals today owe their pleasant lives to the great achievements of the marketplace. "We professors," he says wryly, "are much more beholden to Henry Ford than to the foundation which bears his name and spreads his assets." He also notes that the leaders of the marketplace— businessmen—have personally been strong supporters of the intellectuals, particularly those in the academic world. According to Professor Stigler: "If a professor wishes to denounce aspects of big business, as I have, he will be wise to locate in a school whose trustees are big businessmen, and I have."

Those who view American society as too materialistic—and they unfortunately include too many educators—would do well to absorb Professor Stigler's point that complaints about deficiencies in the public's tastes are misplaced when directed at the marketplace. It is unfair, he says, to criticize the marketplace for fulfilling public desires. "It is like blaming the waiters in restaurants for obesity."

The professor was equally sharp in criticizing the critics who condemn innovations in the marketplace as yielding nothing more than profits for business. "Sears, Roebuck and Company and Montgomery Ward made a good deal of money in the process of improving our rural marketing structure," Professor Stigler said. "But I am convinced that they did more for the poor farmers of America than the sum total of the Federal agricultural support programs of the last 28 years."

My point is that we need a better, unemotional, more realistic evaluation of the respective roles of business, government and education in our free enterprise system. More businessmen need to see that government's concern with the sociological aspects of our economy is highly appropriate. And more government officials and academicians need to see that it is likewise appropriate for business to concern itself primarily with profit, and that their blanket and frequently scathing condemnation of the profit motive, per se, disrupts the very economic process which contributes so much to our social as well as our material well-being.

What all of us need to see—to use academic terms—is that while government majors in social responsibility and business majors in profits, both have a responsibility to carry a vitally important minor in each other's fields.

The ability of American business not only to add material values but even to enhance the quality of life in the United States has been demonstrated unimpeachably over the years. In our time, we have made notable progress in many areas, not the least of which is ethical progress. As Dr. Robert E. Fitch, philosopher, author and student of societies past and present, put it well in a *U.S. News & World Report* interview: "When you compare the large American corporations today with the corporations at the end of World War I, the differences are tremendous. There's a difference in the attitude toward labor, toward the integrity of the product, toward conservation of natural resources, and toward civic and public responsibilities."

A corporation's ethical attitude is the result of its chief executive's beliefs. It reflects the decisions he makes about the kind of company he wants to have. Equally important, the corporation's ethical attitude is a measurement of how effectively the chief executive has communicated his desire for unimpeachable dealings—both by the company and the individuals managing it. It is not enough merely to enunciate a set of high principles. The chief executive must follow through—consistently and forcefully—by establishing procedures which say loud and clear that he will brook no shenanigans, whether in the area of price fixing, conflict of interest, "insiders' information," or whatever.

Whenever a company—or even a single member of its management, however far down the totem pole—is caught off base these days, there is an immediate and resounding clamor in the press. This is exactly as it should be. But both the infrequency and the intensity of such outcries attest to just how far business ethics have progressed in our time.

HOW BUSINESS CONTRIBUTES TO FREEDOM

The times in which we live are such that business and businessmen must contribute still more toward stabilizing the freedom we prize so highly. Just as the architect and engineer must incorporate a factor of safety in designing a skyscraper, a bridge, or a piece of machinery, just so from now on, we managers of American business, if we are to meet our responsibility to the nation—and indeed to the whole free world—must adopt a new factor. We must design into our every product or service, every plan or project, every decision or action, a factor of national security. For unless America can be kept secure and strong, economically and socially, the free world will be unable to stand up against the Communists' aggressive program which still envisages world domination—by them.

That is why literally everything we American businessmen do in the daily discharge of our management responsibilities involves weighing this basic question:

Will it be likely to earn dependable profits, not only to pay stockholders, but also to contribute through taxes to the support of our government, the maintenance of our country's defenses, and our ability to help the emerging nations? For on the ability of American business to make profits depends the preservation not only of our own free enterprise system but of a free world.

This brings me to the last of the motivations which guided my administration of my company for the 11 years I served as its chief executive. I fashioned it as a personal profit-credo, but I would like to share it with you. It has to do with the ultimate goal of the purposeful pursuit of profits and growth, not merely the payment of dividends to stockholders and wages and salaries to a steadily increasing working force, or financing the building of more and more plants and facilities for production and distribution. Rather, it concerns the preservation of a free world.

Let me quote the seven articles of my faith and purpose:

- I believe the world will stay free only so long as this country remains the great leader and example of freedom.
- I believe this country will itself remain free only so long as its free choice system is preserved.
- I believe the free choice system will persevere only so long as our country remains economically sound.

- I believe our country will remain economically sound only so long as its individual businesses are sound.
- I believe its individual businesses will be sound only if they keep on growing and earn profits commensurate with the service they render.
- I believe the profitability and growth of all companies are directly related to the welfare of the country and the preservation of freedom.
- I believe the continued freedom of our country is essential to the preservation of freedom in the world; and I am deeply concerned that my children and granchildren—and all the children and grandchildren of America—shall grow up in a free world.

Surely this is a goal for the pursuit of profits and growth worthy of the best any of us can give to it.